Manzou

慢走

Also By Daniel Skach-Mills

Gold: Daniel Skach-Mills's Greatest Hits, 1990-2000

The Tao of Now

The Hut Beneath the Pine: Tea Poems

In This Forest of Monks

Manzou

POEMS BY

Daniel Skach-Mills

TRANSLATIONS, CALLIGRAPHY, AND ARTWORK BY

Dr. Jiyu Yang

MANZOU

by Daniel Skach-Mills
skachmills@gmail.com

Book design by Dan Lucas
Author photograph by Ilka Kuznik

Printed in the United States of America.

ISBN 978-0-615-90726-0

Acknowledgments

I am grateful to editors of publications where poems first appeared, perhaps in slightly different versions:

Windfall: A Journal of Poetry of Place—"Peak"

"Manzou" was published as a broadside for the Lan Su Chinese Garden *Steeped in Words Tea and Poetry Series*, 2010. It was reprinted in: *In This Forest of Monks* (Daniel Skach-Mills, 2012).

"Sinking Down" was published as a broadside for the Lan Su Chinese Garden *Peach Blossom Spring Poetry Series*, 2011.

My thanks to Solala Towler, editor of *The Empty Vessel: The Journal of Daoist Philosophy and Practice*. *The Empty Vessel* is where I first read about *manzou*. And to Charles Wu who was instrumental in translating the calligraphic inscriptions for Lan Su Chinese Garden in Portland, Oregon.

I am also grateful for Red Pine's translation of: *Poems of the Masters;* and *The Clouds Should Know Me By Now: Buddhist Poet Monks of China*, edited by Red Pine and Mike O'Connor. I am indebted, as well, to Vivien Sung for her book: *Five-fold Happiness: Chinese Concepts of Luck, Prosperity, Longevity, Happiness, and Wealth*. And with much gratitude to Evonne Tang, the teahouse manager at Lan Su Chinese Garden, who assisted me with the Chinese translation in the poem, "What I'll Use In Old Age." Evonne has been inviting me to "smell the fragrance" of all sorts of tea for many years now.

This book is a result of the talent and goodwill of people like Dan Lucas, who designed *Manzou*; and Dr. Jiyu Yang who graciously provided paintings, calligraphy, and Chinese translations (*see:* page 97) to accompany a number of poems. Working with both of you on this project has been like a *yaji*.

For my late Uncle
Peter Bennett
who loved words, sipped his tea slowly,
and who introduced me
to the ancient Chinese poets.

And in loving memory of
Robert Skach.
Like the poet Tao Qian,
you knew the true meaning
of mountains, rivers,
and lakes.

CONTENTS

It is an old and ironic habit of human beings
to run faster when we have lost our way.

—ROLLO MAY

Why settle for super fast when you can have blazing fast?

—WIRELESS INTERNET AD

Introduction

An old Zen story goes like this:

> *A man was strolling by the road when another man sped past him on horseback. "Where are you going in such a hurry?!" the man on the road shouted. From inside the cloud of dust, the man on the galloping horse yelled back: "Don't ask me! Ask the horse!"*

This tale reflects our human condition. Identified solely with thinking, we find ourselves carried off, individually and collectively, by the galloping horse of our conditioned mind. Lost in the dust cloud of our thoughts, we become as out of control as the rider who gives free rein to his steed because he isn't aware that there's anything else he can do, or any other way to be.

Like the man on horseback, most of us really don't know where our frenetic pace is taking us either. Still we cling to it, almost as if possessed. We seem to have bought into the notion that breeding and riding ever-faster horses will get us to where we're going; will get us "there"— wherever *there* is. For many, "there" translates into: *anywhere but here*. Anywhere but where I am at this moment … and as quickly as possible, please!

We are addicted to thinking. And our thinking, which is always wanting more of what it likes quicker and less of what it dislikes faster, can addict us to speed. Thinking and speed go hand-in-hand and, together, have created an electronic technology that is an external manifestation of both. Our racing mind stream is now in the palm of our hand, in front of our eyes, and plugged into our ears. We are assailed from within by mental noise, and from without by a non-stop parade of mind-generated electronic gadgets that focus us outside ourselves and dictate our pace so completely that we are losing our ability to step back, look within, and listen deeply to life. What's more, our compulsive use of these contrivances is, according to recent studies, rewiring our brains; inundating us with stress; and hooking us, not only behaviorally but chemically, on the feel-good shot of dopamine that our brain produces as a reward for answering what might be the next sexual, social, or professional fix pinging from our cyber-device.

Technology can be a practical tool. But, since most of us don't know when or why to say "No" to it, we can wind up mindlessly consuming it until it permeates every facet of our life. Like the Greek youth Narcissus, our mind has become so enthralled staring into the techno-turbid pool of itself that we treat whatever's ringing, vibrating, beeping, or instant-messaging us as more important and worthy of our attention than where we actually are or whom we are physically with. We treat the present moment as if it doesn't exist. And that's tragic because the Now is all we ever really have.

One day a week
can you fast from fast?
untangle yourself from the Internet?
break free from the cell
of your phone?

Enter *manzou*—a Chinese farewell that means: slow down; linger longer; don't hurry off so soon! Never before in human history has this word been more needed. Never before have we been so relentlessly accelerated by blazingly fast Internet speeds, 24/7 wireless connections, and an endless torrent of images and sound "bites" that condition us to rapidly "consume" whatever's set before us. Even the quiet ritual of preparing and sipping tea has been labeled "too time consuming" by advertisers who speed up our pace with *Tea On The Go!* and *All The Benefits Of Green Tea In One Daily Capsule.*

Steeped in this relentless rush, *manzou* is not only a farewell, but can be a welcome homecoming to sanity. Think of it as a pacemaker that can return your racing heart to its original state of balance and oneness with the natural rhythms of the universe, or what the Chinese call "Tao."

One day in seven
can you give your attention
only to the twitter of birds?
the recitation of a sacred text?
a beeper-less page of poetry?

Perhaps nowhere is this invitation to linger longer more evident than inside a Chinese garden. The rocks, water, architecture, scripted poetry and plants are inspiring and beautiful. But even more important than their beauty is their purpose, which is to get you to slow down, relax, and notice what is right in front of you: the sound of rain dripping on banana leaves; the fragrance of tea; a poetic inscription enticing you to listen to the music of plum blossoms; the reflections on lake water that have the power "to still people's minds," as the Tang dynasty poet Chang Ch'ien wrote over one-thousand years ago.

The Chinese poets and sages knew that the world of non-human nature doesn't stimulate a lot of thinking. Yes, for a while you might be wondering what a particular plant or tree is called; or be asking yourself: "Where is that smell coming from?" or "I wonder if I could Google search how long koi live?" But after a while our thinking settles, and a felt sense of oneness with life (what some call "being") takes center stage. The result? "After an hour here I feel like I've had a massage!" was what one woman told me after taking one of my tours at Lan Su Chinese Garden in Portland, Oregon.

I have wondered for years if the Garden may have had the stilling effect on this woman's mind that Chang Ch'ien refers to in his poem. From a holistic perspective it is certainly no secret that when the mind slows down, the body—as this woman was quick to notice—loves it, and relaxes.

Feeling your life takes time.
One day will you? Can you?

True, everyone isn't fortunate enough to have a Chinese garden in their backyard the way we do in Portland. Which is why, dear reader, these poems (many inspired by Portland's Chinese garden) are here for you. Use them to create a sane niche for yourself, wherever you are. Think of them as a first step on what the Chinese poet Chang Jian called, "the meandering pathway leading to the deep recess" that is your inner life. Although slowing down is not explicitly mentioned in all the poems here, it is *implicitly* present as the internal pace out of which the words strolled onto the page. Saunter with them, meander alongside them. Sit and ponder when you need to, move on when it feels right. There is no hurry here. No race, no rush. Only Tao, the deeper current of life itself, waiting as it always has for you to pace yourself to the rhythm of the way things actually are. *Manzou!*

—Daniel Skach-Mills

A TRAIL FOR OTHERS TO FOLLOW

The soft overcomes the hard.
The slow overtakes the fast.

—LAO-TZU

Snail

Slow, your pace is this poem finding its way,
antennae reaching, always reaching,
the scripted shell of every word
concealing as much
as it reveals.

Small, you inch your cursive crawl
line by wandering line
across the tightly ruled page of our vision,
leave in your foot's filigreed wake
a trail for others to follow;
a shine.

Glint

Unable to sleep, I set my pen to paper.
Hours later, a poem's last line has yet to arrive.
In light this dim, don't we all stumble around like stanzas,
searching for what comes next to complete us,
feeling our way toward one another slowly in the dark?
Nodding off, I wake to find dawn's rays
illuminating the empty space on the page
where the verse's ending still eludes.
No matter. Hasn't waking
to what can't be said
always been a poet's job?
translating the glint
of first light
into words?

Staying Centered in the Urban Center

Only when we linger do we touch the sacred.

– *Rainer Maria Rilke*

Trilling birds wake me in the morning.
Chirring crickets lull me to sleep at night.
Days unfold slowly enough for poems.
Evenings arrive quietly enough for tea.

Outside my garden gate:
people rushing around,
eyes glued to screens,
ears plugged with wires.
No longer noticing
trees or flowers,
deaf to the music
of birds and rain—
what madness!

Thank heaven
that I paced my life years ago
to drifting clouds and plum blossoms,
allowed myself to lag at leisure
behind current trends.

What a blessing that I can't think
of anything faster than blooming roses,
have nowhere to get to sooner than moss.
That I can't remember when I last gasped
for tomorrow's breath today.

Wu Wei

You cannot rush the rose,
cannot force its secret scent
to tell, disclose, reveal,
no matter how much
you stomp and yell,
harangue or cajole.

Get as red in the face as it is
it will not bloom to all your bluster,
can wait as long as love takes
for you to deadhead yourself of demands;
for your fists furled tightly
into what florists call *bullets*—
buds of hothouse flame
that will not open fire—
to flower.

Little Surprise

the way we speak the names
of the dead out loud in our sleep,
run fingertips slowly over their handwriting,
signatures on faded letters,
startled by the indelible ink
of what's here, yet not here.

How, cracking books,
we find what we didn't lose—
pressed rose petals opening again,
red as lipstick kisses between
our shared love of words,
pages we never bothered to read,
my mouth tasting the years
they bookmarked with fragrance
for the very first time.

Turning, Again

My temples tinted white,
and it's not even winter.
Vine maples mottled yellow,
though it's not yet fall.

Before long,
branches will be bare again.
In a few short years,
everything my arms hold dear
will be gone.

Seasons outside
seasons inside—
where do they come from,
and where are they going?

Cascading
over my gaiwan's rim,
tea returns me
like a waterfall
to still pools
in the mountains.

步入蒼翠中的茶樓坐到一張老木
桌邊陽光透過秋楓紅葉正好灑灑
落在了桌面靠在刻有壽楓的清式
椅上周遭繞著宜人的遠山近水頓令
身邊的憂慮拋在腦後就象唐朝
蕭蕭灑灑的李白胡子沾上了薄薄的秋霜
要知道這茶壺裡的嫩葉其自比我
多活三千年的老樹　史聞淼"黃昏"
癸巳秋日於茶園寶山楊[illegible]小宇書

Taking Tea In Autumn

Stepping into the teahouse at dusk,
I choose a rosewood table the sunset shade
of crimson maple leaves, my usual Qing chair
carved with longevity peaches.
Somewhere amid mountains and lakes
I left behind worries about old age—
my beard, hoary as autumn frost, just like Li Pai's.
My tea grown from trees that have lived
thirty times longer than I will.

Peak

After Yang Wan-li (1127-1206)

Snow on the summit thicker than last year,
or even the year before that. And I'm not
even talking about a mountain!

Now, it's descending to the lower elevations:
drifts clinging to the overhang of my chin,
the sloping hills of my chest.

Hands folded at daybreak, bowing to the east,
how long before I'm the spitting image
of old Mount Hood?

Wrinkled face slipping in and out
of fog's shifting memory,
my peak on earth reached.

In Loving Memory of Robert Skach (1921-2013)

What Appears For You At The End Through A Window Of Providence

will outlive us all—
Mount Hood's western face beckoning you
to become this final kiss of sunset
pressed to its craggy cheek,
the limpid eyes of mountain lakes
reflecting your life's fading alpenglow,
tongues of soughing fir whispering you
back into trees, winters when silence
was the only thing snow had to say.

It's what comes for you now,
steadfast, like a brother or a friend,
your years stepping forward
into the millennia of its embrace
without leaving a single track,
the hidden deer of last things
leading you deep into understory,
thicket-ing you from our sight.

Look—it's a mountain's way, isn't it?
To never let on which side is other.
To lift our burden of raised questions
pointedly into clouds,
wisps vanishing like your hair
on the summit
where beauty and dying
both take our breath away.

Dispersion

No wind.
Bamboo outside my window
stands perfectly still.
Years roll by like clouds.
My poems go unread.
Alive, a poet's work
is seldom noticed.
Dead, you stand a small,
but slightly better chance.
Outside my door this morning,
the three sticks of incense I light
fill the air with fragrance
whether anyone
smells them
or not.

Looking Up Leisurely I See …

pink cherry blossoms
never falling quite like this
before or again

Slow

This garden meanders.
Paths that would take me three steps
to traverse elsewhere,
here, they take me nine.

Bulbs sprout up when they're ready.
Persimmons fall when they're ripe.

At one with the true pace of things
I linger, happy as a fish
that swims contentedly
in the space it's been given.
That doesn't have a clue
what thirst is.

THE EFFORTLESS GLIDE

Fish forget that they live in the water.
People forget that they live in the Tao.

—CONFUCIUS

Sinking Down

Tower of Cosmic Reflections Teahouse

The fish's grace relaxes tension.
The waterfall's song goes well with tea.
Koi in the lake sink slowly to the bottom.
Leaves in my cup float briefly on the top.
What starts out on the surface here
always returns to what's deeper.

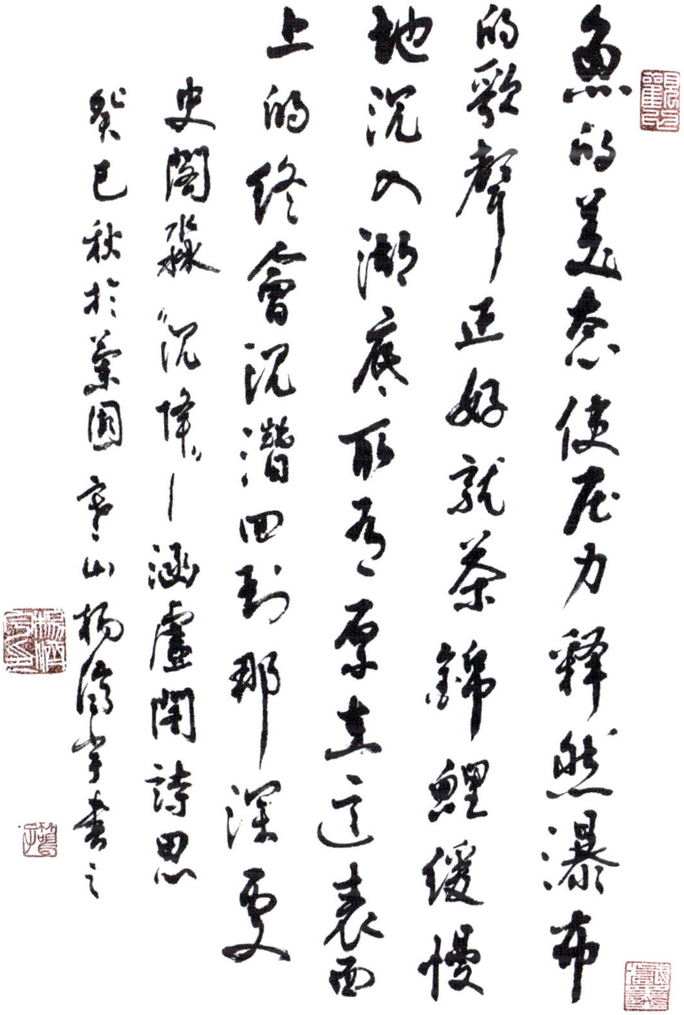
魚的羞態使尼力釋然瀑布
的歌聲正好就茶錦鯉緩慢
地沉入湖底形為厚重這表面
上的終會沉潛回到那深處
史闇楓〈沉偉〉—涵盧閣詩思
癸巳秋於葉園 寧山楊修寫書之

Watching People Watch Koi

Lan Su Chinese Garden – Portland, Oregon

What hooks me,
catches my pen's undulating cursive
without barb or fail
is how quickly the onlookers relax,
the body's taut lines slackening
as thoughts sink down;
as koi— swimming up through
the twin tributaries of the legs,
the care-dammed backwater of the face—
spawn, in the media-muddied
meres of their eyes,
this pool of clear seeing
where, like a fish,
the effortless glide of who they are
rises silently, for a moment,
to the surface.

During T'ai Chi Class I Recall The Film: *A River Runs Through It*

A Confucian sits on the bank and studies the river.
A Taoist jumps in and splashes around.

To move as the movie's titled
is why we are here—
thirsty to wend again
as creek, rivulet, brook;
as life stream rather than mind stream,
effluent without effort
and our constant flood of thoughts,
the endless eddying around
those early submerged stones:

Sit up *straight!*
Get in *line!*
Try *harder!*

all blocking
the deeper undercurrent
we know is us:

blood *stream*
spinal *fluid*
urinary *flow*

wading the Way
back into where we're dammed
until our wrists become rills
the torso: trickle
arms: arroyos.

Until our flesh resurfaces
as what it's always been:
body of water
bubbling up from beneath
all our heavy layers of mind
into current, cascade,
a river's love
of letting.

View

Teahouse doors and water lilies opening onto the lake.
Dragonflies and swallows both flying, but not the same.
Katsura leaves, this time of year, can't even imagine yellow.
Hibiscus, this time tomorrow, won't remember pink.
Sipping tea, how strange it feels to see the goldfish
swimming between the heron's legs
and not be able to warn them.

雨珠點點落在湖上茶葉片片墜在杯中池塘的水清澈而靜在鷺鷥灰暗身影下瞬間浪花飛珠四濺魚和茶壺都沒了水

史聞淼淼空空摘錄

癸巳秋於菜蘇園寶山楊滄宇書之

Empty

Drops of rain stippling the swollen lake.
Beads of tea dotting my empty bowl.
Beneath the heron's still gray shadow, the ripples are clear.
With one splash, fish and teakettle are both out of water.

A Poem Written While Birds Of Prey Soar Over Qin Lake

Red-and-gold leaves circling on top of the water.
Orange-and-black koi undulating beneath the waves.

Never confusing leaves with fish,
the heron sees clear through
to the lake bottom.

Distinguishing thoughts
from who and what she is,
the Master plumbs the depths
of her own mind.

Furling the short wingspan
of what you think you know,
can you dive like the osprey
that breaks through what's surface
to feed on what it loves?

葉子在池上飄浮魚兒在水中戲游
高高立湖上盤旋的魚鷹一眼那清澈的
湖水隨即落在湖邊立定這老鳥心懷鬼
胎地盤算忽然收緊了短短的翅夫傍人
自然猜着了下一幕能想像出這兇狠的
鳥兒驟然把嘴插入水中捕獲了所愛的美
味

史閱琛《琴湖觀鳥》—魚鷹立湖上句報的詩意

癸巳之秋於葉蘇園寶山楊[illegible]寧書之

Reflections

Strolling the lake shore at twilight
I linger where we first met,
still hoping to find you there.
Like waves in the water,
decades come and go.
Like reflections on the surface,
memories appear, then fade.
Shining down on me through the willow,
even the moon's bright lamp
can't help me find
where I've misplaced
the years.

Pausing On The Lakeside Terrace Of The Lotus Hall

After Yang Wan-Li

An August breeze sways the lotus flowers.
Carried away by so much beauty,
even the dragonfly's unable
to settle on a single bloom.
Rooted deeply beneath the surface,
do our loves ever really grow old?
Gazing into still lake water,
my white beard is just another
passing cloud.

漫妙輕柔的音樂兮令詩人飄飄欲仙沖泡得恰
好的茶水能使俗者神寧心靜人神情致合一之感
又何人可說道清楚之緣為何我吮吸著芳香那柔風送
是那箏聲抖落了松針上的露珠
癸巳夏日

Oneness

A well-played tune can lift a poet's spirits.
A skillfully prepared tea can quiet a person's mind.
This oneness I feel—who can explain it?
The hummingbird sipping at the same time I do.
The wind—or is it the zheng?—glissando-ing
raindrops from the pine.

Paradox

There is a deep Quiet
that isn't disquieted
by noise

a supreme Stillness
that remains unmoved
by movement

a natural Rhythm to things
that cannot be disrupted
by human frenzy

There is great paradox
in this world

soft growth appears
from hard wooden branches
hard rain falls
from soft puffy clouds

There is as much coming together
in any given moment
as there is falling apart

The Master has been living
as the space between these movements
for a hundred-thousand years

STANDING IN YOUR OWN SHADE

My internal pace is slow.
Mine is the slowness of the tree
that embodies its growth and its blossoming.
Mine is the concealed slowness
that conceives and gives birth
to every work of art.

—RAINER MARIA RILKE

Where The Master Stands

Pace yourself to the rhythms of the Tao
and you will see the truth—

> birth is you
> life is you
> death is you

See the truth, and you will perceive the Oneness—

> sound is silence that's become audible
> activity is stillness that's taken on movement
> form is formlessness arising out of
> and returning to itself

Perceive the Oneness, and what is there to fear?

> The Master sees the world as himself
> Seeing the world as himself,
> what could he possibly want
> that's not what he already is?
> People don't understand him
> He is like a tree rooted
> in a depth of knowing others cannot see
> He has stepped out from under
> all the voices that would have kept him
> from standing in his own shade

Somewhere Near Your Hermitage I Remember You But Forget The Way

Where trees and deep shade merge
my mind wanders to you,
a recluse living in these hills.
Once, I knew by heart
the way to your hermitage;
but that was years ago.
Shadows my only companions
I climb now to where the trail ends,
just high enough to glimpse mist
swirling up like incense from the valley floor.
Ahead, a fir grove sways in autumn wind.
Behind, a mountain range stands in setting sun.
A wild deer, who can say where
you dwell now?
among clouds, perhaps—
or like this stone sitting motionless
amid pine duff and crickets,
your monk's robe indistinguishable
from tree bark or snowfall,
a forest's slow weave
of lichen and moss.

By Myself

After Hui Ch'ung

A day indoors
I linger over tea, books,
a poem's unfinished stanza.

Content with little,
rarely in a hurry,
haven't these always been
the secrets of a happy life?

Long parted
from cloister garths and monks,
my mind hangs like the bell
in empty space
over Guadalupe Abbey.

Listening To The Waterfall, I Remember The Abbey Bell

Where in the waterfall's cascading cadence
can you detect past or future?
Where in an ocean wave's ebb and flow
can you glimpse a single mistake?
Snow embraces everything it touches.
Plum blossoms fall wherever wind decides.
Slowing down, you catch up to what I'm saying.
Speeding up, you fall behind.
The human world can drive you crazy
if you let it. Be like a bell,
that fills the air with clarity
by emptying itself
of its own sound.

Manzou

Abandoning trails east of the abbey, I head into dusky woods.
Cicada's trill marks a turn. A shaft of setting sunlight
arrows where to stop and notice the pine.
Deer slip silently into the bracken.
The bell fades quietly into the trees.
Unless you've paced your life to manzou,
you won't understand my walking stick
beating me again to the shrine on the hill.

Shrine

The clouds overhead aren't going anywhere.
The road under my feet has already arrived.
Stopping at the shrine, the ant on Pu T'ai's belly
doesn't know that everywhere it steps is Buddha.

頭上的流雲
無邊無際
腳下的旅途
正在等待
走神壇邊上
找些止步
布袋和尚
瞇眼中的
不會明白！
無論怎地
都無法逃脫
佛祖的掌心
癸巳夏

You Are That

The poet is on the side of undeceiving the world.
—Seamus Heaney (1939-2013)

So why do we leave the lights on, anyway,
except to snuff our fear, illumine the way
for hope, coming home later
than we expected,
to find us?

Truth be told,
hasn't the switch we're searching for
always been right at our fingertips?
the power to return to Kansas
(or wherever it is we're standing)
undimmed by all our mental toggling
between opposites like *On* and *Off*—
or, for that matter, enlightenment
which (as any Ch'an Master knows)
is simply the bulb of your head
unscrewed from the belief that there's a *you*
to be enlightened or unenlightened,
the frayed cord of the self being pulled,
in a flash, right out of our sockets
is just one more way life keeps
plugging us into darkness,
the sudden shock of having nothing
visible to kneel or prostrate to—
no tabernacles or reliquaries,
stupas, or Wall Street with its other Dao
if that's where you believe the Sublime lives.
Nothing "out there" to bow to,
but only out of any one
of the myriad power boxes

short-circuiting us from seeing
the light of our own divinity;
the tacit conspiracy Watts called:
the taboo against knowing who you are,
which keeps us from recognizing and embracing
that the thousand-armed Guan Yin
seated full lotus on the altar is *You*,
the truth so fragile She holds it for us
in Her peacock fan of porcelain hands,
no charge, until we're ready,
just a little offering of tea, incense,
(a bargain, really) what's holy
always way under-priced,
yet costing everything.
Always right under our feet,
and our Feet, too.

Yes, I have difficulty
holding what I'm saying as well,
my hands fumbling to grasp
the weight of that much lightness—
that *You are that which you are seeking*
as Saint Francis said
is just one more reason to stand still
and notice what it feels like
to be held sacred by gravity;
to bend and then break the rules
at your own waist
by bowing to this world as yourself.
To move slowly and,
when you do,
toward.

Root

Wisdom comes from living life deeply, not quickly.

Stepping out of the city's clamor into my garden's calm,
I wander at ease beneath pine trees filtering sunlight,
camellia flowers dripping rain.
No longer focused on departure or arrival
no longer rushing to get from here to there
busy people hurrying by
might glance at me and wonder:
am I a mountain, a cloud,
or an ancient root
deepening?

Recluse

Here in my little garden I sit contentedly,
hidden amid bamboo and pine.
Orchids bloom in summer.
Chrysanthemums appear in fall.
A recluse at heart, my gate shut,
who can turn away the visiting scent
of star jasmine?

Scatter

I used to believe
in borders and countries,
land parcels and plots—
but that was before my fifty-sixth November
when the colorful flags of leaves
draped their silent anthems of disregard
across all our straight-talking fences,
our perfectly pronounced property lines.

US soil? Canadian? French? Chinese?
since when does birth require
a visa to enter this world?
death, a passport to leave?
What citizenship did the ancient sages
lay claim to, wandering like deer
Hsieh Ling-yun's poetically rendered
ridgelines and stanza-silted streams?
his mist-bound massifs
blurring every distinction between
self and other,
this side or that.

Autumn, yours are the windblown boundaries
I'll defend. When I pledge allegiance,
let it be to your passing color guard's
renegade reds and golds;
your desegregating
scatter.

Spent

Another autumn.
My youth—where has it gone?
Everywhere, bare trees stand witness
to a lifetime of partings.
Chrysanthemums bloom and fade by the roadside
whether anyone notices them or not.
Rich, poor, who can surpass
the generosity of aspens
spending their last gold coins
on the wind?

Leaving

Teahouse nearly deserted.
Katsura almost bare.
These somber autumn days—
what are they filled with but emptiness?
Sitting alone, my cup steeped
only with memories,
this falling yellow leaf
leaving the last one behind
is more than my heart
can bear.

池塘裏盡霧裡
太陽躲在雲中
即使年紀大了 許多事
都還是想不清楚
秋葉從樹上落下
那是什麼樹都無從想起
錦鯉身上的紫和彩斑
緣何要如此組合
都總是無從解釋
—秋日水邊

Strolling Along The Water On A Fall Day

Wispy fog veiling the garden pond.
Heavy clouds blanketing this morning's light.
Even in old age, so much remains unclear—
autumn leaves fall from a tree
whose name I don't remember,
and koi match the colors
in a way I can't explain.

Wang Wei's Way

Snow doesn't care how long it takes
to hide the familiar landscape from our eyes,
how deep it has to go to cover all our stories.
Recreating mountains, trees, it's an artist, isn't it?
the way each flake always comes down to what's here,
first things first, its blank white scroll unrolling
slowly across all our names for things is, after all,
what the old Tang painters were getting at,
their soaring brushstrokes landing black as crows
in the hush of the rice paper's empty field
so little for the mind to feed on, really—
two, maybe three beaks tops
pecking the words right out of our mouths,
Wang Wei's way with ink silently translating
the peaks of all our lofty questions into fog,
a trail's winding tongue disappearing into clouds.
Even the road's old familiar answer
vanishing snowbound beneath your feet
isn't really such a bad thing, is it?
The relentless blizzard of thoughts about
where you've come from
and where you're heading
left with nowhere to go but here,
no directions where to find you.

Winter Morning

After Chia Tao's "Overnight At A Buddhist Mountain Monastery"
Lan Su Chinese Garden—Portland, Oregon

Dawn-tinged pavilions
surround the fog-covered lake;
a view the garden teahouse faces.

Darting hummingbirds
weave green into leafless branches;
clouds soar one direction,
crows the other.

Few people seem able
to linger anymore;
the phoenix no longer
rests in the trees.

Reclusive as a monk,
an old koi
cloistered only by pine shadows
has never inhaled a speck
of the world's red dust.

Poem Written On A Wakeful Winter Night

Gusting into the wee hours,
what does this sleepless winter wind know
about our need to lay to rest
the steady ache of aging aspirations,
our burden of burned-out bones?
its jointless chill more skilled
than mice or sparrows
at finding cracks in the house.

Approaching the dawn of sixty,
don't we all wake to find
our dreams dropping away, one by one,
beneath the same gray cloud cover
as maples in the yard?
limbs so empty they can hold
the moon and stars;
their grasp on nothing
revealing the whole sky.

What I'll Use In Old Age

A dictionary that undefines everything,
slows my years of looking up down,
the world sighing relief
from a park bench
at being allowed, finally,
to rest in what it is,
to speak for itself.

After seventy, the only teacup I use will be Yixing,
and way too small to hold all our noise,
our overflowing pot of information.
On the cup's unglazed face:
no logos or mobile apps,
web addresses or links
to anywhere but here,
anywhere but where I am.
Only the two Chinese characters
my eyes will incise invisibly
into the clay's sienna surface—
wen xiang: smell the fragrance.

It's enough, don't you think?
to inhale and not say anything—
no subject or object,
no over-steeping in nouns
which, as we age,
are the first to go
anyway.

To use getting old
as my departure from description;
as the silencing that it is
of my tongue's ode to opinions,
adjectives, all the ways
of pronouncing
what I am not.

Looking Inside

My Yixing bowl's
thin porcelain lining
pops with an audible *ping*
when I pour in the tea.
Cracks and lines appear
where before there were none.
Gazing into its fissured bottom,
how could I not recognize
my own aging face
peering back at me?
this fragile breaking through
of the inner life
I drink from.

宜興茶壺薄陶胎滚水注入

SIPPING ANOTHER WORLD

I want to grasp time in my hands,
raise it to my lips,
speak to it of slow,
whisper to it of more.

—NATHANAEL GRAY, OSB

Tea Monk

When I arrived at Lan Su Yuan, all my cares ceased.
A gaiwan is too small to hold any worries.
A poet is too poor to invest in sleepless nights.
No longer in the cloister, but still a monk at heart,
who could have guessed that I'd wind up here,
with thick clouds for my robe
and a tea bowl for my monastery?

每當進入茶蘇花園所有心事便會釋然這盞碗實在太小容不下那許多的憂慮詩人也實在窮花了錢過多的不眠之夜不在修道室裡禪坐內心仍是一介僧人誰又可以理解得到為何我會定居於此泥雲作袍茶碗化緣

史閑林"茶僧" 癸巳秋寶山[illegible]書

Gazing At "Ten Thousand Ravines In Thick Clouds" Through A Window In The Four-Sided Hall

My window frames ancient mountains—
cloudy crags and jagged scarps towering above deep ravines.
Such heights! at my age I've abandoned dreams
of reaching them, my days inclined now
to nothing steeper than high chat,
this vertical drop of oolong cascading from my Yixing pot.
Truly, just living with a view of peaks like this
can change a person's heart forever.
What need then to go searching for my walking stick?
my battered trekking shoes?
Only people lost in the fog of separation
see things as close or far.

On Hearing The Zheng Being Played In The Garden On A Spring Day

White clouds rising like mountains in the southern sky.
Pale blossoms falling like snow outside the northern wall.
Wafting on a gentle breeze, from which immortal's heaven
have these sounds from the guzheng come?
notes strumming wavelets across the surface of the water,
tones reverberating lake-shimmers on the undersides of leaves,
their otherworldly song plucking
this poet's heartstrings like *Tao Hua Yuan*,
resonating a lifetime of longing
without intoning a single word.

一瓶橙黃色鬱金香、花苞掉地落
於桌上 茶壺中的葉子緩緩展開散漫
出沁人的馥馥芬芳 獨自悠然飲著嗅著
味道別人無從知曉 太和天地原是冷
暖自知 史閑詠 — 冷暖自知
癸巳夏 濟宇寫之

Nothing Is More Obvious Than The Hidden

A vase of orange tulips
dropping petals onto the table.
My teapot's terra cotta spout
blooming fragrance into the sky.
Here, alone, no one knows
what flavor of tea I'm drinking.
Since the beginning,
hasn't heaven on earth
always favored
hiddenness?

While Sitting In The Teahouse Another World Appears

After Tim Barnes' "One Country Before Sleep"

Most of life's evils arise from humanity's inability to sit still in a room. —*Pascal*

Here, the ink flows so slow
that the poems of Li Po and Du Fu
are still being written.

Trees bend in autumn wind, and by
the time they've straightened, it's spring.

Days don't run on time; they meander
like gardens, amble on trails.

Tea saunters out of pots steeped
with hours so generous they never run out,
and the local college requires a course in sipping
that lasts an entire semester.

Yes, there are still words here that aren't still—
archaic terms like *hectic* and *hurry*, *frenzy* and *rush*
that no tongue in town can bring forward
from that far back in the mouth
to pronounce.

Here, clocks tell time in a language
no one speaks, and the only date on the calendar
is the one you have with your life.

Old men linger so long
playing dominoes in the park
their moves look almost like seasons.

And when someone dies,
the people gather the slow pace
of that person's life lovingly into their arms,

set it down between them, and wait
for those years still strolling
contentedly beyond time
to happen.

Song

For Dan Lucas
After Tom Crawford's "Bird Walk"

No, not the dynasty—

although that golden-tailed-bird
of-an-era in China
can still make us slow down,
turn our heads round one-thousand years
to do a double-take on beauty—

but only the old men strolling today,
hands behind their backs
beneath the always abundant snowfall
of white hair in Shanghai,
their arms no longer reaching
ahead of them for anything

unless, of course, it's to embrace
the caged finches and canaries
they bring to *Renmin Gongyuan*,
The People's Park, where they perch
for hours, dozing on benches
while the city molts hurriedly past them,
indifferent mostly to what they hold so dear—
the small bird of the heart
pressed fluttering against the chest,
love's rib-caged song
that refuses to be
held inside.

In A Ch'an Buddhist's Backyard

Wisdom? Let go of what you think
and you'll glimpse it,
right there behind the house:
the bird—warbler, maybe, or a finch—
that sees the shadow of the feeder
silhouetted against the wall
but doesn't try to eat from it.

By the shed, too—
aren't the empty flower pot and bucket
both Tao before we hurry
to fill them with words?
the wheelbarrow turned over
so completely to *being* rust
that it can't hold an intelligent
conversation *about* rust.

Even compassion
when you spot it here
looks the same as it does in all our yards—
trees never pulling themselves out
from under any bird;
willow limbs graceful
as Guan Yin's countless arms
withholding shade
from no one.

Cloak

For my late Uncle Peter Bennett

"See—he's sharing his warmth
with his dog," you say,
directing my barely hewn
twelve-year-old attention
to the carved rosewood Qing figure
centered on your coffee table,
a Ch'an monk seated on the ground,
his canine's nacre eyes
peeking out from under
the embrace of his left arm,
a rush cloak covering
both their backs.

Forty-five years gone,
and the closest I've come to China, uncle,
is this stateside teahouse I'm sitting in
scratching out verses between teapots and cups,
my enjambment dovetailing not nearly as well
as the Ming latticework framing the windows,
this view of storm-swayed hills.
Wind, rain, whichever way you look here
life's still the same old bark and whine
about weather we can't control,
the age-old huddle against
indifference, cold.

Today I'd like to sit
and brew gongfu tea with you
while sipping verses
from Pound's *Cathay*,
the Song and Tang poets
you loved so well.
You, who worked in lumber mills,
plywood glue rooms,
your hands sharpening saws by day,
honing poems by night.

Tall, thin, of English descent,
you moved slowly through
this world's fog-covered fen,
a graceful crane,
your stride hidden
by rushes and reeds,
years I keep parting
to glimpse you,
their tattered cloak
covering you in
windblown decades,
and me, like the
dog.

Making My Way To The Garden Teahouse In Winter Snowfall

After Han-Shan Te-Ch'ing

The city's pace slows, and traffic noise softens.
Inside the garden's whitewashed walls
the plum blossom and I are the only ones here.
Snow on the granite bridge isn't trying
to get from one side to the other.
Drifts covering the courtyard floor
reveal no human tracks.
Allowing this moment to fall wherever it falls,
my flurrying thoughts settle, then vanish
like snowflakes touching the lake.
My gaiwan's sloping white lid
is a snowcapped peak
hidden in deep clouds.

Cha Tao Ren

Descartes said: "I think, therefore I am." A Ch'an student says: "I am, therefore I think." The Master hears the word "I" used twice in the same sentence, and laughs out loud.

Our thinking mind won't save us.
Didn't Einstein try to tell us this?
You won't find solutions
using the same tool
that created the problems
or something like that—
words not being that important either
when it comes to what's real,
our name, phylum, class, category
for the red-crested
we-really-don't-know-what-it-is
perched on the fence
is just one more takeoff
from what's right in front of us,
another flight from mystery
the universe doesn't believe in.

I think, therefore I am.
Now there's a death sentence.
Poor Descartes. He didn't
look deeply enough,
didn't have enough tea in him
as the Chinese are wont to say,
mistaking, as he did, the tiny bowl
of his head, filled to the brim,

for the empty pot that holds it all;
the void within that Lao-tzu said:
makes the vessel useful.

You have to see it the way
the old Taoist sages did—
humanity not separate from anything,
the Chinese character for the word *tea*
steeping us—*ren*, the ideogram for *person*—
right here between the terra-rooted
radicals for *trees* and *grass*.

Ren—
the character that resembles
an upside down V,
two sticks like a pitched tent
supported by the earth,
propping each other up.
Two leaning as one into this world
(that's all I'm trying to say here)
where everything is us.
Where everything depends.

GLOSSARY/NOTES

Cha Tao Ren: means "way of tea person." In Taoism, there are many "ways" to re-realize your oneness with what the Chinese call "Tao." The spiritual practice of properly preparing and presenting tea is just one of these "ways."

Ch'an: the syncretism of Taoism and Mahayana Buddhism in China that later became Zen in Japan.

Confucian: a person who follows the teachings of Confucius which emphasize self-control, adherence to a social hierarchy, and observance of civic rules and protocols as a way to bring order to society.

Dao *see:* Tao.

Descartes: René Descartes, the 17th century French philosopher whose famous dictum "I think, therefore I am" placed the capstone on the west's identification with cognition alone as a "self." Descartes' philosophy drove the final wedge of separation between matter and consciousness/subject and object into the western psyche. This Cartesian dualism between what's "in my head" (me) and what's "out there" (the environment and so-called "others") has left many in the west feeling disconnected from the planet and a felt sense of oneness with life. (Note: other philosophers contemporary with Descartes did refute his claims. It is my opinion that because their views weren't as politically and economically advantageous as Descartes'— especially to those European countries that had espoused both colonialism and environmental domination—their philosophies didn't rise to the top.)

Du Fu: (aka Tu Fu) along with Li Pai, one of the most famous poets of the Tang dynasty (618-907 CE).

Filled to the brim: in the Chinese tea ceremony, the cups are never filled completely. This is a symbolic reminder that the human mind is also like a bowl that should never be filled to the brim or, even less desirable, overflowing with thinking.

Four-Sided Hall *see:* Lotus Hall.

Gaiwan: a tea bowl with a saucer and a lid.

Garth: a small courtyard.

Gongfu: means "art" or "skill." Gongfu tea is the art of preparing and presenting tea.

Guadalupe Abbey: a cloistered Roman Catholic Trappist Monastery, thirty miles southwest of Portland, Oregon. I was a monk here from 1987 until 1992.

Guan Yin: the Chinese goddess/bodhisattva of compassion and mercy. Guan Yin is sometimes depicted as having one-thousand arms which allow her to embrace the world's suffering at every moment.

Guzheng: a Chinese zither.

Happy as a fish: from the famous Chinese story *The Happiness of Fish*, in which the Taoist sage Chuang-tzu says to his friend Hui-tzu as they're walking along the river, "I think the fish look really happy today."

High chat: (aka "pure chat") philosophical wit or banter based on the writings of Lao-tzu and Chuang-tzu that originated with Ch'an monks around 300 CE, and later became popular among the Chinese literati.

Hsieh Ling-yun (385-433 CE): a recluse, and China's first "rivers and mountains" poet.

Hui Ch'ung: a poet and landscape painter of the Song dynasty. The last stanza in my poem *By Myself* was inspired by the last stanza in his poem *Given to Wen Chao* where he writes, "Long parted from pine forests and vines/my mind hangs in space/over King's Chamber Mountain."

Lan Su Yuan: means "garden of awakening orchids," the poetic name of the Classical Chinese Garden in Portland, Oregon.

Lao-tzu: the Chinese Taoist sage who is reputed to have written and/or compiled the *Tao Te Ching*, or *The Book of the Virtue of the Way* in the 5th century BCE. Chapter 11 of the *Tao Te Ching* reads: "We shape clay into a bowl, but it is the bowl's emptiness that makes it useful."

Li Pai: (aka Li Po) a famous Chinese poet of the Tang dynasty (618-907 CE). The reference to "autumn frost" comes from his poem, *Chiupu River Song*.

Longevity peaches: in Chinese folklore, a fairy goddess, the Queen Mother of the West, gave the Han dynasty emperor, Wu Di, peaches of long life from trees in her magic garden. Longevity peaches are actually steamed buns shaped like peaches that are filled with red bean, date, or lotus-seed paste.

Lotus Hall: a lakeside building at Lan Su Chinese Garden in Portland, Oregon. (Also called "The Four-Sided Hall" because the four walls consist entirely of see-through windows.)

Manzou: (pronounced "mawn-zoe") the Chinese farewell that means: slow down; linger longer; don't hurry off in such a rush!

Mountains and clouds: the domain of Taoist sages and hermits. Many Taoist hermits lived on peaks so high above the clouds that they came to be known as "cloud walkers." Clouds also represent wandering monks.

Mount Hood: a dormant volcanic peak east of Portland, Oregon. The Native American name for the mountain is "Wy'east."

Nacre: mother-of-pearl.

Nothing Is More Obvious Than The Hidden: a line from a poem by Chung Yung.

OSB: stands for *Order of Saint Benedict.* Nathanael Gray was a Benedictine monk who gave me a packet of his poetry just prior to his departure from the monastery in the mid to late 1980s. He died in the 1990s. This epigraph is from one of his untitled poems.

Phoenix: the mythical bird in China that represents the empress. It is often seen in Chinese art with the Chinese dragon. It is said that the phoenix will only land in a parasol tree when a ruler comes who brings peace and justice to the land. During his lifetime the Chinese philosopher, Confucius, lamented that he never once saw a phoenix land.

Pound's *Cathay*: a translation of Li Pai's poems by American poet Ezra Pound (1885-1972).

Power to return to Kansas: in the film *The Wizard of Oz*, Glinda, the good witch of the North, speaks like a true spiritual Master when she states that Dorothy has always had the power to leave Oz and return home to Kansas. How often do we keep looking on the outside for what will bring us home to ourselves?

Pu T'ai: in Taoism: the fat, laughing Buddha with a huge round stomach. Also known as "Hotei" in Japan.

Qin Lake: (pronounced "chin" lake) the poetic name of the lake at Lan Su Chinese Garden in Portland, Oregon. The qin is an ancient musical instrument that resembles a zither. Smaller than the guzheng, the qin's origins date back three-thousand years.

Qing: (pronounced "ching") the Qing dynasty (1644-1911 CE).

Red dust: the world of human affairs that can lead us to compromise our values and principles in order to obtain wealth, fame, status, and power. In Buddhism: the world of the senses.

Reliquary(ies): a container or shrine where the bones of saints or holy people are kept.

Rewiring our brains: see: *iCrazy—Panic, Depression, Psychosis. How Connection Addiction Is Rewiring Our Brains. Newsweek*, July 16, 2012.

Rush cloak: poor itinerant monks often wore cloaks or capes made of woven rushes or straw.

Song: (also spelled "Sung") the Song dynasty (960-1279 CE) during which science, philosophy, and the arts in China thrived.

Tang: the Tang dynasty (618-907 CE).

T'ai Chi: a form of exercise characterized by slow rhythmic movements patterned on the movements in nature, especially the flow of water. Based in Chinese medicine, T'ai Chi optimizes health by keeping the energy pathways (or meridians) in the body clear.

Tao: (pronounced "dow") sometimes spelled "Dao," it means "way" or "path." Although Tao cannot be conceptualized, it is present as the rhythmic, cyclic flow of nature that we witness both around and within us. Awakening to and aligning yourself with this deeper current of life, rather than your egoic mind, is primary in Taoism which de-emphasizes intellectual and academic prowess in favor of intuition, felt experience, and "not-knowing." This "via negativa" (or "negative way" as it is called in the west) is the doorway to a deeper way of knowing. Tao becomes available to our perception when we are aligned with what *is* happening, rather than our belief in our thoughts *about* what is happening.

Tao Qian (365-427): a Chinese poet who, after reveling in the wonders of nature one day, wrote: "Amid mountains and lakes lies the true meaning. I try to express it, but forget the words."

Taoist: a person who uses Taoist spiritual practices and principles as a way to live simply and in harmony with the natural course of things.

Tao Hua Yuan: (pronounced "dow wah you-when") means "Peach Blossom Spring," a mythical land of peace and plenty in Chinese mythology and folklore.

Ten Thousand Ravines In Thick Clouds: the poetic name of the mountain range at Lan Su Chinese Garden in Portland, Oregon.

Thick clouds for my robe: "thick clouds" was inspired by *Ten Thousand Ravines In Thick Clouds*, the poetic name of the mountain range at Lan Su Chinese Garden.

Tower of Cosmic Reflections: the poetic name of the teahouse at Lan Su Chinese Garden.

24/7: twenty-four-hours-a-day, seven days a week.

Understory: the smaller trees and shrubs that grow beneath the larger trees in a forest.

Wall Street with its other Dao: Dow Jones and Company, Inc.

Wang Wei: a famous Tang dynasty (618-907 CE) poet and accomplished landscape painter.

Watts: Alan Watts (1915-1973) the late Asia scholar, philosopher, Episcopalian minister, and self-proclaimed "spiritual entertainer" who wrote many books, including: *The Book: On the Taboo Against Knowing Who You Are*. Watts firmly believed that the wisdom of the Taoist sages held the cure for the ills of the west.

Way *see:* Tao.

Wild deer: hermits in China were often referred to as "wild deer."

Willow: symbolizes affectionate bonding because of how the long branches twine around one another. Willow branches or catkins were often given to a friend or loved one in parting.

Window Of Providence: Providence Hospital in Portland, Oregon; but also a window through which guidance from God or nature comes (in many spiritual traditions the two have not been separated). My father-in-law, Robert Skach, enjoyed a seventy-year relationship with Mount Hood, a dormant volcanic peak east of Portland, where he skied, fished, and built a family cabin. "Providentially," the eighth-floor hospital room he was moved to just prior to his death had a large window that looked east toward Mount Hood.

Wu Wei: probably the most misunderstood Taoist principle in the west. It is usually translated "not doing," but a better translation is "not forcing"—not forcing things to happen or not happen. Wu-wei is about skillfully navigating life rather than waging war against it, or wasting your energy trying to push or pull the river in the direction your egoic mind thinks it should go. The current flows along perfectly without your having to think about it, thank you very much. Or, as a Zen master once said when asked to describe enlightenment: "Spring comes, and the grass grows by itself."

Yaji: a gathering of Chinese scholar-artists.

Yixing: (pronounced "ee-shing") also called "purple sand clay." Yixing clay comes from eastern China and has been used to make Yixing teapots since the Song dynasty (960-1279 CE).

Zheng: (abbreviation of "guzheng") a Chinese zither.

TRANSLATIONS

Taking Tea In Autumn (Dusk) 黃昏

步入黃昏中的茶樓
坐到一張老木桌邊
陽光透過秋楓紅葉
正好洒落在了桌面
靠在刻有壽桃的清式椅上
周遭繞著宜人的遠山近水
頓令年邁的憂慮拋在腦後
就像唐朝蕭洒的李太白
胡子染上了薄薄的秋霜
要知道這茶壺裡的嫩葉
來自比我多活三千年的老樹

Slow 慢

花園蘇醒了
別處三步走過的小徑
這裡卻慢度了九步
花芽到時會破土的
柿子熟透時自會拍地落下
與那行事怱促者比我悠然
就像魚兒一樣自在
（不像心浮氣燥的人們
而只在自有的空間
心安自得地悠游著
不必為飢渴而操心）

Dispersion 消散

在那無風的靜謐裡
窗外綠竹悠悠不動
我的詩照平常到來
猶如過眼煙雲
當然無人吟詠
活著－
詩人的作品鮮受注目
往生－
或許還會有些少機會
今早門外點了三柱香
是否有人聞到香氣
那實在是無關緊要

Sinking Down 沉降

涵虛閣詩思

魚的美態使壓力釋然
瀑布的歌聲正好就茶
錦鯉緩慢地沉入湖底
茶葉在杯裡向上翻升
所有原在這表面上的
終會沉降回到那深處

View 近景

茶樓門開　湖上花開
新燕和蜻蜓各自翻飛
今年樹上未見嫩黃的葉芽
木槿花明日此時定未變紅
啜著清茶懷著怪異的感覺
遙望著那金黃色的魚兒們
在那兇狠的鷺鷥的長腿下
仍然那樣地悠來游去
卻無法警告它們小心

A Poem Written While Birds Of Prey Soar Over Qin Lake 魚鷹在琴湖盤旋勾起的詩意

葉子在池上飄浮
魚兒在水中戲游
高高在湖上盤旋的魚鷹
一眼看穿那清沏的湖水
旋而降落在湖水上立定
這老鳥心懷鬼胎地盤算
忽然收緊了短短的翼尖
傍人自然猜著了下一幕
能想像出這兇狠的鳥兒
驟然把嘴撞入水中
捕獲了所愛的美味

Empty 空

雨珠點點落在湖上
茶葉片片掇在杯中
池塘的水清沏死靜
在鷺鷥灰暗身影下
瞬間浪花水珠四濺
魚和茶壺都沒了水

Oneness 合一

漫妙輕奏着的琴音
可使詩人飄飄欲仙
沖泡得恰好的茶水
能令俗者心靜神宁
人神情致合一之感
又何人可說道得清
蜂鳥同我吮吸芬芳
是那柔風還是箏聲
抖落了松針上的露珠？

Manzou 慢走

沿寺院向東的荒涼小道
步向那陰森的樹林
啲啲蟬聲引我拐了個灣
這時面向的是夕陽
一縷光線穿透進來
陽光停在了一棵松樹
野鹿滑入路邊的厥叢
禪鐘忽然消失在林中
除非生活的步履能放慢
否則無法明白我的柱杖
緣何又趕著我走向山上的神壇

Spent 消耗

又是一夏
我的青春都到了何方
隨處的禿樹就是寫照
猶如今生今世的離逝
小菊在路邊開了又謝
不管是否有人在注意
窮的富的從邊上走過
只有那慷概的白楊樹
風中花光了最後一文

Shrine 神壇

頭上的沉雲無邊無際
腳下的路途正在等待
在神壇邊上拽然止步
布袋和尚臍眼中的蚁蝼
怎會明白　無论怎地
都無法逃出佛祖的掌心

Strolling Along The Water On A Fall Day 秋日水邊

池塘裹在霧裡
太陽躲在雲中
即使年紀大了
許多事卻還想不清楚
秋葉不斷從樹上飄落
叫甚麼樹卻無從想起
錦鯉身上調和的彩斑
緣何如此組合
總是無從解釋

Looking Inside 沉思

宜興茶壺薄陶胎
滾水注入茶花開
戰戰抖抖叮叮響
淡淡紋路顯出來
如鏡返照自憐面
始知人生須釋懷

Nothing Is More Obvious Than The Hidden 冷暖自知

一瓶橙黃色鬱金香
花苞拍地落在桌上
茶壺中的葉子緩緩展開
散漫出沁人的裊裊芬芳
獨自悠然飲著啜著
味道別人無從知曉
太初
天地原是冷暖自知

Tea Monk 茶僧

每當進入蘭蘇花園
所有心事便都釋然
這蓋碗實在是太小
容不下那許多憂慮
詩人也實在是太窮
花不起過多不眠夜
不在修道室裡禪坐
心裡仍是一介僧人
誰又可以理解得到
緣何我會定居於此
沉雲作袍
茶碗化緣

Daniel Skach-Mills is an award-winning poet, author, and a former Trappist monk. His poetry has been published in a broad spectrum of journals and anthologies ranging from *Sufi* magazine and *The Journal of Daoist Philosophy and Practice* to *The Christian Science Monitor* and *Sojourners*. He is the author of four previous books: a chapbook, *Gold: Daniel Skach-Mills's Greatest Hits, 1990-2000* was published by Pudding House in 2001; *The Tao of Now* (Ken Arnold Books, 2008) was listed by *Poetry Northwest* editor David Biespiel and Oregon State Librarian Jim Scheppke as one of the "150 outstanding Oregon poetry books" for Oregon's sesquicentennial in 2009; *The Hut Beneath the Pine: Tea Poems* was a finalist for the 2012 Oregon Book Award (judge: Carl Phillips); and *In This Forest of Monks* ranked as a double finalist in both the Poetry and Spirituality categories of the 2013 Next Generation Indie Book Awards (judge in Poetry: Kenneth Salzmann; judge in Spirituality: Richard Cook), and was described as "a powerful work that touches, delights, and amazes" by the judge of the 21st Annual Writer's Digest Book Awards.

Daniel holds an undergraduate degree in Religious Studies from Marylhurst University, Marylhurst, Oregon; and a graduate degree in Counseling Psychology from St. Martin's University in Lacey, Washington. A docent for Lan Su Chinese Garden since 2005, he currently lives with his partner of twenty-one years in Portland, Oregon.

Dr. Jiyu Yang received his Ed.D. from the University of Northern Iowa. He was the chairman of The Association of Children's Intellectual Development in Guangxi, China, and has done extensive research on music education and children's intellectual development.

Currently he lives in Portland, Oregon, where he teaches music, leads The Orchids and Bamboo music ensemble, and serves as the head of The Wisdom Arts Academy. He is also one of the standing directors for The Oregon Chinese Art Association.

Dr. Yang frequently lectures on Chinese art, music, calligraphy, and poetry at universities and colleges in Portland and south Washington state.

Dr. Yang was recently invited to Italy to give a lecture and workshop on Chinese art and calligraphy, and to give erhu concerts. He traveled throughout Italy, France, and England to visit art and music schools and to study at the great museums there.

25757652R00073

Made in the USA
Charleston, SC
13 January 2014